Travel/ Travail

Poems

by

Thomas Zimmerman

ISBN: 978-93-90601-54-7

First Edition: 2022
Rs. 200/-

Cyberwit.net
HIG 45 Kaushambi Kunj, Kalindipuram
Allahabad - 211011 (U.P.) India
http://www.cyberwit.net
Tel: +(91) 9415091004
E-mail: info@cyberwit.net

Acknowledgments

The author thanks the editors of the following publications, where these poems first appeared, sometimes in earlier versions:

Abandoned Towers; *Acts of Resilience*; *Antiphon*; *The Arkansan Review*; *Big River Poetry Review*; *The Big Windows Review*; *Bigger Stones*; *Black Elephant; Blood Orange*; *Blue Fifth Review*; *Brickplight*; *Califragile*; *Carcinogenic Poetry*; *Cellar Roots*; *The Corner Club Press*; *Curio Poetry*; *Dead Snakes*; *Driftwood Bay*; *The Drunken Llama*; *Epigraph*; *Eyeflash Poetry Journal*; *The Flea*; *Furtive Dalliance*; *Hermes Poetry Journal*; *Hunnybee*; *Inner & Outer Spaces*; *The Lake*; *Leaves of Ink*; *Lost River*; *Lyre Lyre*; *Man in the Street*; *The Maynard*; *The Meadowland Review*; *The Midwest Coast Review*; *Milk Sugar*; *Motley Press*; *Nice Cage*; *Nine Muses Poetry*; *On Becoming Real: Six Sonnets*; *Origins*; *Outside In Literary and Travel Magazine*; *The Pangolin Review*; *Parks & Points*; *Peeking Cat*; *The Petrichor Review*; *Political World*; *Poor Mojo's Almanac(k)*; *Poydras Review*; *Pulsebeat Poetry Journal*; *Pyrokinection*; *The Rain, Party, & Disaster Society*; *Rasputin: A Poetry Thread*; *The Road Not Taken: A Journal of Formal Poetry*; *The Rotary Dial*; *The Sacred Cow*; *Sledgehammer*; *The Sonneteer*; *Soor Ploom Press*; *Steel Moon Publishing*; *Summer Reading/Crossing Borders*; *Telling Stories*; *These Lines*; *Time Zones Lit Review*; *Tipton Poetry Journal*; *Trestle Ties*; *Wandering*; *The Wayfarer*; *Yellow Mama*; *Zingara Poet*.

Cover image by the author. Author photograph by Monica Cialek.

Contents

I. North America 7

Crooked Highways 8
Trip 9
After Burying My Mother 11
Rivers and Trees 12
Mississippi 13
At the Collier Mansion 14
America's Pastime 15
Hotel Lincoln Blues, Chicago 16
Peach Fuzz 17
At Starved Rock State Park 18
Shelter 19
Bob Dylan's Singing 20
Broken Record 21
Blue Ballpoint 22
Compensatory Consumerism in Cleveland 23
The Gift-Bearer 24
Road Trip 25
Stars Adorn Our Ankles 26
Deep Montana 27
Geyser 28
Tetons Journal 29
San Francisco Symphony 31
Temporary Crown 32
Channeling the Anasazi 33
Rio Grande: A Fragment 34
Orange Cat 35
Stuck Inside of Louisville with the Dayton Blues Again 36

First Time in Florida 37
Eternal Surf 38
Seaside 39
Prince George Hotel Blues, Halifax 40
Chanty 41
Bigger Than a Country 42
Henceforth 43
A Little Song 44

II. France 45

Tramping: Paris 46
From a Garret in Paris 47
Americans in Paris 48
Pont du Gard 49
From a Balcony in Nice 50
Aquarium 51
The Guide 52

III. Greece 53

Alive and Breathing in Thessaloniki 54
Postcards from Athens 56
Socrates Sandals 57
Dionysus and Apollo 58
After Visiting Mycenae 59
Note from Arachova 60
A Note on Craft 61
Note from the Peloponnese 62
Mind in Flight 63
The Glory That Was 64
Ottoman Dreams 65

IV. Italy 67

Notes from Rome 68

Cypresses 70
Pisan Protest 71
Venice 72
In the Shadow of Vesuvius 73
Italian Sonnet: I Think of Us 74
Rubble-Song 75

V. Great Britain 77

Highland Fling 78
Glasgow Necropolis 79
Americans in Oxford 81

VI. Conjugal Journeys 83

Conjugal Journeys 84

I.

North America

Crooked Highways

Tonight, beers two-thirds gone, just like our lives,
I contemplate senility. "My groove's

become a rut," I say, a line I wrote
so many years ago. "Relax," you say,

"there's Dylan on the stereo." *Relax.*
It's always Now. My mantras. Comforting

but trite. The wind's just right: I hear the tires
whining on the interstate. Bob too:

"I've walked and I've crawled on six crooked highways."
Traveling, we've loved to play this game:

we see a weird car, or weird people
in a roadside bar, and one of us

will ask the other, "Wonder where they're going?"
How many times we've asked it of ourselves.

Trip

We're driving west on 94, through Michigan,
a nip of Indiana, 80 west, Chicago,

boring deep past Dixon, Ronald Reagan's birthplace,
farms, old neighborhoods down on their knees, some others

belly up. Election year, police and race,
division, subdivisions, deportation, radicalization,

"I am bad, but not as bad as my opponent,"
virus biting babies, women cracking ceilings,

gender fluid/flowing, family a reconstruction
reconstructing. Mississippi River, Mississippi

Fred McDowell is on the stereo: "I do not play
no rock 'n' roll," all twang guitar and nasal rage,

Black artist from the South who signifies for more
than just himself. Our privilege, it makes this easy.

Easier. Now Iowa. White-bread Dubuque in '91
was luring Blacks to integrate. Well-meaning but

wrongheaded, so the papers said. On US 61,
I think of Dylan and the shifting versions of

the '60s. Those assassinations then have left us leaderless
till even now. Next exit, Cedar Rapids. Then

Lost Nation. Haven't been there yet. The wind turbines
like spaceships landed in the rolling hills, like mills

of childless gods. We head in the direction of
the devil, north, to Anamosa Prison, Zwingle:

pastoral we pass, that's passing, past. This bridge
will take us to the Land of Lincoln. That one, to

Wisconsin. Let's pull over, get some chicken, beer.
Your mother's waiting. Nothing else is going to stop.

After Burying My Mother

for MJZ 1939-2009

Wind-turbines' three arms whirling, slicing like
they'll walk the earth before they scrape it clean:

we're driving near Des Moines, see three, then ten,
eleven: sci-fi eerie as *The Day*

the Earth Stood Still. My wife and sister sit
in back, there's Elvis on the radio;

and mirrored rows of corn and beans, green fields
that roll like moon-chained Gloucester surf that yields

to nothing human. Boston's years ago.
The rest-home interregnum banished it,

with vodka and MS's aid: the way
that choice and chance efface the who/what/when/

where/why, the way the crooner's voice, so keen,
fades fast unless he's standing at the mic.

Rivers and Trees

The Avon, Huron, Arno, Tiber, Thames:
some rivers I have seen but never swum.
The banyan, mangrove, breadfruit, rubber, gum:
these northern hands have never touched their stems.
But I remember young and drunken love
beside the purling Nishnabotna once.
Mosquitoes bit my ass; I was a dunce
to teenage lust, but blessed. A mourning dove
perched cooing yesterday within our burled
crab apple tree; our neighbors' orange cat
lay coiled beneath. No, I'm no Adam; you're
no Eve—but we have eaten tree-fruits that
both cleared our eyes and numbed our lives. Our world
is flux: a river fouled, then spring-fed, pure.

Mississippi

I'm rolling on and on, the river's slow,
three states in sight, the smell of fish, of mud,
the taste of salt, wildflowers in my blood.
I used to fear the water. Oh, not now.
Lots under here. The blackest beast, of course,
is all I need. The time will come—I hope
I'll know—when I'll be torn to pieces, then
put back together whole, with duct tape, rope,
the plants and herbs I'll newly know, like gorse
and vetch, the witches' broom, verbena, hen
and chickens. Hurt is on that stereo,
my mind. Sublime, so I don't get the whole.
My thought of God's like this. You play your role,
embrace the ambiguity, let go.

At the Collier Mansion

Brown skeletons awaiting better days:
the way we see the trees. Friends stoking us
with coffee in the morning, beer at night.
Good morrow, and good morrow, and good morrow:
chugging like full tugboats. Cell phone photos
of the Mississippi River snapped quick
from the car: they slide across my mind,
chunked blue ice blurred by motion, sun, like aging
eyes, or stars on windy nights. Infinity
still undiminished: loss gapes wide, then morphs
into discovery. Let's face the whole,
be done with crossing out. Great sex this morning,
Catholic wake this evening. Family from
the south and west descend: this house sleeps ten.

America's Pastime

I drank a half-gallon of beer
at the Cubs game today. Home
team won with three in the ninth.
Ninety degrees, great seats,
high and in the shade, along
the third-base line. Booty-
song on the radio there: *I'm all
about that bass.* Fair enough.
Is the anima erupting, as my friend
William insists? Is global warming
our fault? Is suffering ever
earned? Imponderables. Don't get
too damned wise. The beer was strong,
the shade was cool, and I had three
people I love sitting with me.
I watched my niece's purse and diet
coke while she looked for the women's room.

Hotel Lincoln Blues, Chicago

So someone's bashed in Volvo, Honda, Jeep,
and Buick windows all along the street.
I'm back from breakfast, burping pork and sweet
preserves: not sure what fruit they were. The creep
who sat behind you eyed your ass. *It's mine*,
my glance declared. We knew I lied. There *is*
a devil. Suns his loins, then takes a whiz
in Lincoln Park. He's not Miltonic. Fine:
that makes him more a schlump, like me each time
I try to write a poem or make a move.
The cops and cabs whoosh by below, you're on
the phone, your mother's dying slow, I mime
the act of travel-writing. God, our groove
was back when you were wrapped around me. Now it's gone.

Peach Fuzz

The harvest moon, my dear, is God's ass when
we're coming down from high or buzz with three-
day stubble. Call it love. Reactors' glow:
your breasts. And I'm a toxic spill. But will
it last? You used to tell me I was closed,
my poetry was constipated: dry-
turd verse. I've tried so hard to loosen up,
bolts moaning, hinges whinging. Yes, it's just
a vision that we're whole. You've *got* a hole:
thank God for that. Let's get back in the car
and gobble up more miles. "Play anything
but Dylan. . . . I was *joking*." So you say.
We're crossing borders that the money's made:
past truck stops, peep shows, toll gates, cop blockades.
Our ever-reimagined love-song, "Life
Is Just a Slow Slow Death," still radiates
above the interstate, breaks over us in waves.

At Starved Rock State Park

The milkweed floats like jellyfish in air,
but there's no sting: it's only ghosts that make
us wheeze. I squeeze your shoulder, but your stare
says, "No, not yet." I walk behind, mistake
the rhythmic cling-release of cotton on
your hips for bedroom curtains once in Nice,
Laguna Beach, or Bath. I want to catch
you like a fish, but when will you release
me? Meadow grass was ocean once, and dawn
revealed, beneath the sway of dinosaur,
beneath some trembling leaf, a rodent: this
was über-papa, our progenitor.
Your mouse-brown hair is clinging—let me snatch
it—there—from just behind your ear, and kiss.

Shelter

Baudelaire lies steaming on the bedside table.
Dylan sang hard rain on us from Davenport
to Battle Creek. A storm a guest without
departure date, and shelter just a curtain
caught between the claps. We taste the solubility
of skin in air, of words in silence. Neighbors'
houses melting slowly down the blocks,
like butter lambs in frying pans. Chorizo
and Manchego on the cutting board.
Green grapes, cheap burgundy, the harder stuff
I'll want to hit so soon: all cool as pillows
in long marriages. We've fizzed like salmon
in the river, hugged the driftwood in
the flood, been lost, thought drowned, grown legs, been found.

Bob Dylan's Singing

July 8, 2017

Tyler, Zach, and I, Joe Louis Arena,
Detroit: and outlaw Bob's a crooner, propped
behind a not-so-grand piano that
he dearly beats to death. He's butchered "Tangled
Up in Blue," and now we're straining hard:
Hmm, what's this tune? He's 76. He thinks
he's 34. A simple twist of fate,
let's say. I say, *say* some*thing*. Plead with those
whose affect's flattened. Flatter with affection.
Smoke rolls off my heart like fog from that
machine beside the stage. Have I found beauty
in a stranger place? *Oh. Frank Sinatra.*

Broken Record

for AZ

But that ol' way don't work no mo', an earworm
blues insists, the spell like one of John Lee
Hooker's, cooking slowly, spices biting
psyche, inciting flesh. I wish I were
with you. Instead, a horseshoe booth, brewpub
snuggery, midtown Detroit, with Zach
and Tyler, three-headed monster talking music,
poetry, and social justice. God help us.
Change will come, like backyard birdsong, northern
woods' boot-sucking mud, the wandering planets
in the blood. The waitress brings me Belgian
ale, my third. I text you pictures of
the record-pressing plant we've visited.
It's retro chic, producing art that spins like wheels.

Blue Ballpoint

This blue ballpoint, it glides just like my tongue
between your breasts in better days, on wilder
nights. And, oh, to moor in thee, as Emily
exclaims. But such allusions dog us. I
am listening to Archie Shepp, his Coltrane
homage not as edgy as I'll bet
it was in '64. That year I lived
in Turkey, army brat whose mom was hot
enough to get her ass pinched by the locals
in the market. Later, Dad in Vietnam,
the '60s spooling out like torn intestines.
Crack a few less beers, and love the world
a little more, I want to tell you two,
you three, you four. You're dead. It's why I write.

Compensatory Consumerism in Cleveland

Hilton Garden Inn, 2:15 am

Buying stuff
to justify our drudgery.
At the Greenhouse Tavern,
tuna medium-rare
w/ three black IPAs,
then new black coat
rained on hard,
front-seat small-talk
w/ African cabbie
who rescued us
so we over-tipped.
More beer later at Harvey's Bar—
talked *Hamlet*, baseball, &
authenticity
w/ an anthropologist &
two philosophers.
When one went to bed,
the rest of us divvied up
the beer he left.
Blew all my cash:
instincts right, can't do math.

Note to self:
Next time you want to go, stay home.

Note I predict I'll write tomorrow:
Never believe a drunk.

The Gift-Bearer

This silver pendant's like an icicle
or spike, a thing that she could kill me with:
the gift hurled back to bearer, as in myth.
Oh, moping in Ohio's farcical:
she's in Ann Arbor now. My three-beer buzz
has drugged my psyche's guards to let me brood
on weaknesses, to rouse the demon mood
that fouls my *am*, my *will be*, *could be*, *was*.
The earrings that I've bought are shaped like shields.
She'll wear them for protection: not from me,
but from some crack in me she sees that yields
abysses old as Homer's wine-dark sea,
as ghost-enraptured Hamlet's, home from school.
The rest of me is Yorick, Hamlet's fool.

Road Trip

The interstate's alive with whining
tires tonight. The sun's chugged back
to Santa Fe, there's Tom Waits on
the stereo, and choirs of crickets
mating in the grass. To stay
in place is negligence. Chicago's
five fast hours away, the Mississippi
less than eight. So hook your bra,
zip up your dress: we're heading west,
as far as we can drive on vodka,
coffee, chewing gum, and rest-stop
sex. We're not too young to gnaw
the rind of weird old America,
to test the strength of self-
mythology, to find what Whitman,
Kerouac, and Dylan blessed,
a dreamscape horny, mad, poetic, kind.

Stars Adorn Our Ankles

Magnetic is the dark abyss, and strong
the wind on northern plains, the land so flat,
the sky so big that, nights, the stars adorn
our ankles. "Veils of topsoil," reads a poem
I wrote in North Dakota, "dancing black
and naked for the plaid-backed farmers." You
were lying on that hotel bed, in shock
on our arrival, TV chained against
the ceiling, stars around *its* ankles. Blue
as atlas interstates, crabbed veins adorn
my ankles now, and so much laid out flat
behind, beside, in front, inside, of me:
my mother grown into a hoop I keep
on jumping through, my father's eyes the earth
so torn it blurs the far horizon line.

Deep Montana

We've stepped into a pool of silence. Deep
Montana. Haze from distant fires. High
up there, above the treeline: speck of white.
A mountain goat? A patch of snow? Won't know
unless it moves. We've eaten huckleberries,
thimbleberries, heard we could survive
on old man's beard in dire times. We've seen
a black bear flipping stones along the shore
of Waterton. Bald eagle. Osprey. Bighorn
rams have butted heads before our eyes
at Logan Pass, the sound a muted gunshot.
Later, ewes and kids, fifteen or twenty,
trotted past us at Two Medicine.
As if we needed proof that we were healed.

Geyser

We drank four fingers' width of Idaho
potato vodka, wolfed a hamburger,
slugged beer below the Tetons. Horses begged
like dogs for French fries, mom and daughter, brown
as burning earth and melting with the flow
of images, kaleidoscopic blur
before/behind our eyes. Half-drunk, we legged
it up a switchback on a cliff-face, down
a canyon. Rainbow falls, wildflowers, pines:
each axis vertical, so we could glide
to paradise or slide to hell, the roof
of which we walked in Yellowstone, with lines
of pilgrims, faithfully, to see a fried
white angel flee the earth, redemption's proof.

Tetons Journal

1
The Tetons off the balcony—
like me,
awash in blue-gray haze.

I drank an oak-aged IPA
at Wolfgang Puck's in Denver.
Read Baudelaire,
Detroit to Jackson Hole.

I stuck my head inside
a teepee.

Feel affinities.

2
Snake River rafting,
saw bald eagles, ospreys.

Great blue heron in a marsh.
And ravens everywhere.

A bull moose in the brush.
Some huckleberry vodka.
Stayed astride
a horse named Buster.

Cowboy sang while rainclouds sat
on Mount Moran.

3

That roof in Moose, Wyoming:
good for drinking beer.

It's Idaho beyond
the eastern slope:
the mountains craggy, close, most beautiful
I've ever seen.

The *Tetons*.
First fur traders named them:
French for *breasts*.
Gets lonely in the West.

San Francisco Symphony

From Alcatraz, we watched Blue Angel jets
that spiraled, rolled, and dove in sea-blue sky
above the bay. We bought a book by Bly
at City Lights. We sent e-mail regrets
to colleagues, saying we'd be out of touch.
We rode the bus down Haight and back to paw
used jazz and folk and punk CDs. We saw
some Painted Ladies, ate and drank too much.
We scaled Nob Hill to catch Van Morrison's
Masonic Temple show: all scat and blues
and Celtic soul. We dodged the Wharf, the views
from Lombard Street, from Telegraph. The fun's
the moment—now—as well as memory.
We heard the San Francisco Symphony.

Temporary Crown

Union Square Marriott, San Francisco

Slight toothache from this temporary crown
can't stop my worried peanut-munching ways
and makes elixir of this wine I down,
the heel of last night's drunken screw-top haze.
Tonight, my wife is in the other bed—
the two in here are neither king nor queen—
so I, this chain-hotel's Macbeth, my head
a-swim with symphony we've heard and seen,
will be denied the chance to murder sleep
with any hapless sex advance. Perhaps
the ferry-ride to Alcatraz, the steep
Nob Hill ascent to Chinatown, our map's
equivocation took their toll. A pawn
in marriage, I will dream as king till dawn.

Channeling the Anasazi

We took the gravel road off Highway 4,
northwest of Santa Fe, to reach Tsankawi:
prehistoric Anasazi pueblo
village.
            Clouds hung low, the Jemez Mountains
sawed at the horizon, earth and stone
glowed orange-blue: no other humans there.

We hiked the mesa, climbed the ladders, stooped
within the dwellings scooped out of the cliffs,
saw petroglyphs. But this was seventeen years
ago: no photographs, just memories
that drift like smoke in wind.
                                        I felt the spirits
there. *Your reading and your mythic bent*
just conjured this, my Western mind's kept telling
me.
        I crease a journal page, I've tried
to leave my record.
                                    So, what drove those people
there? What made them disappear? We
can answer feebly but more feelingly
as schism and pandemic scatter us.

Rio Grande: A Fragment

The Rio Grande's a dirty string between
McAllen and Reynosa. So I thought,
the times I made the crossing south in '82.
Saw dogs on spits in merchants' windows,
roasting and rotating. (Goats, I realized
later.) Drank Tecate in the streets,
gave money to the first few begging children,
bought my girlfriend necklaces, a cotton
dress of burgundy: embroidered birds
and blossoms on the bodice. Spoke a little
Spanish there, but couldn't conjugate
my verbs as quickly as self-consciousness
could tolerate. One trip I took was with
a friend from high school days, his fiancée,
and parents too. We drank a lot at lunch,
dad argued with the waiter, then the manager,
about the cost of margarita pitchers:
lost, and paid in full, of course. Up north
was weirder. I taught school, leased a bungalow,
no heat or air, papaya tree in front
and lime trees in the back. Two turkeys roosted
under my Ford Galaxie 500,
windshield spider-cracked. My alcoholic
landlord in a trailer right next door.
He drank a case a day of Texas Pride.
The case is what he sat on in the shade,
no shirt, would lift his rump when he was empty.
Someday I'll tell you about his wife.

Orange Cat

That orange cat my wife calls Tom has just
soft-shoed across the deck. Half-stray, a boarder
on our porch most nights, he's fire in silhouette
against our massive shaggy spruces.
Where's his witch? I think of Texas and
my addled landlords there who named two pet
wild turkeys after Ann and me. The husband
drank the contents of the case of beer
he sat on every day outside their trailer
home. His wife tried several times to jump
my bones when all of us were drunk on Texas
Pride (a brand of beer, I swear). Home-dyed
her hair, had rotten taste in men. A neighbor
told me that she'd never had a man
who tried to please her. Said he'd offered once
to suck her toes and warned me that the husband
kept a loaded shotgun. Women! Men!
Sweet mystery! My first love was a redhead.

Stuck Inside of Louisville with the Dayton Blues Again

Fairfield Inn and Suites, 12:15 a.m.

The floor-lamp's fizzy, spinning
molecules and atoms into
orbitals as wild as bourbon in the throat,
as King Lear's fool's *bons mots*,
which Brian and I, half-
drunk, self-styled Shakespeareans,
ingested at the bar: the Seelbach
Hilton, Scott Fitzgerald's muse
for part of *Gatsby*. Three Dog Night,
the star attraction down
on Fourth Street, sang a blues-
and-Bud-Lite pop we didn't hear.
Game Two was on the television:
Cardinals and Red Sox. I will botch
the poems I read tomorrow
at the conference. But need I care?
Right now, if I sang madrigals
in Dayton, there'd be strippers
I could woo.

First Time in Florida

I ate a sloppy joe at Sloppy Joe's,
the Key West bar that still-young Hemingway
got drunk in every day. I wrote no prose
but drank each night to coax the muse to stay.

I held a four-foot alligator in
the Everglades: the keeper kept him cool
and dull, a rubber band around his thin
toothed snout. I? Pink and grinning like a fool.

I picked up shells along a Gulf Coast beach:
the lightning whelk, the fighting conch, the clam;
saw dolphins cutting through the scud; heard screech
of gull and boom of surf. I never swam.

A tourist only viewing life, you see?
It's what I was, and am. Will always be.

Eternal Surf

Marco Island, Florida

The outdoor pool's a heated 81—
about the normal mood and age round here—
and on the beach, bikini top undone,
a spray-tanned coed's drunk on sun and beer.
I walk the sand with eyes cast down for shells,
but see just scales and fronds and blobs; a mat-
furred quadruped; a flesh-pink hunk that swells
then shrinks in sun. I loathe my belly-fat.
The blue waves ripple white, a Quaker's beard;
at night, the surf's a birthing mother's moan,
and all that buried life's still there, still feared,
despite the scotch, the iPod's soothing drone.
At times, the ocean smells of death, so old,
so choked. But never dead—no, not that cold.

Seaside

How water slaps the dock! A gull careens.
Could be Laguna, or Rehoboth, Beach:
the hotel-room pastels, the harbor scenes
gilt-framed, the sea-smell balcony, a peach,
some brie beside the sweating bucket, wine
half gone. How many times have we been here?
The sea churns up so many things: a line
of verse, some beached and squiggly thing to fear,
the ancient roar and moan of birth and death,
remembered sex, of course, that straddles both.
Asleep or waking, I am here but loath
to wade in deep, though tides have pulled me, breath
and sight bereft, to realms of consciousness
my mind will alternately curse and bless.

Prince George Hotel Blues, Halifax

The TV news: a power plant's destroyed,
a kidnapper's been killed, the hostage safe.
The telephone sits silent, ruin void
of visitors. My shirt and lanyard chafe
my sunburned arms and neck. Those garden beers
were worth the pain: an IPA, a strong
brown ale. And then we walked along the piers,
the harbor boozy blue, each noisy throng
of tourists buying, grazing, gaping—just
like us. Right now, the sun is swording through
the drapes. The king-size bed's a mess—it must
be love. And now you've left me: "Got to do
my hair and put my face on straight." Who says?
We won't be back to work for seven days.

Chanty

I never knew I was so small until
I started thinking. Then I saw the sea,
and since, such drinking. Silly stuff to ease
the labor. Makes me think of mothers, sea
inside them serious as origins.
Like you, I was a whale that swallowed all
until I walked. At Plymouth Rock, so near
my mother's home, I ate rock candy, deep-
fried clams. I've read my Melville too, seen
whales erupt from glassy froth like revenants
from graves, converted lobster boat we sat
in bobbing like a tin cup on the Bay
of Fundy. Now, red sky that signals warning.
Or delight—Love, sing with me tonight.

Bigger Than a Country

We gobble up the road: the window blurs
with fields and trees, with billboards and the lake
below the bridge. Remember that we're pass-
ing through, so "Howdy, unearned suffering,"
and "Cancer, will you sign my dance card?" Got
our passports? Here's the border. Duty-free
is next: Bacardi, Bailey's, musty beer
in bottles that we can't return. They'll check
the trunk. Have we released that hostage yet?
We call it love. Don't lose the car keys. No
one here is ever going home again.

Henceforth

Last night, the motel buzzed with snowmobiles
and Escanaba bowlers. Dorm-warm room
beside the stairs. It's years since we've been north.
Free breakfast ends at 10. The TV's on.
Get dressed. Our friends are happy here. It feels
like art should be as brief as life: the bloom
bad-ass and wild as wolf or bear. *Henceforth*
sounds dead—but it's just old, like petals, dawn,
migrations of the flocks and herds. The *now*'s
still there, not buried—planted, ever fresh
with [place your beautiful abstraction here].
Beneath the awning, howls of wind. I browse
my memories: part webby mess, part mesh.
Get dressed. The snow is melting, sky is clear.

A Little Song

Houghton Lake, Michigan

The clouds have lifted, voices sweeter, deep
inside my head: it's you, O Muse, come down
to help me write a little song to keep
me sane. This cabin fever: far from town,
I read, I paint, do push-ups, knee-bends, eat
as healthy as I can, but drink too much.
A microcosm of my life, complete
with wife who cleans and dog that sleeps, my crutch
of industry: I'm keeping busy, need
to work, to feel the joy my parents made
me with, and for. The trees are swaying, freed
of leaves, their dun-brown shifting sun and shade:
a mirror of a rooted, balanced me,
alive, attuned to change eternally.

II.

France

Tramping: Paris

We tramped along, across the Seine, got sprayed
by Paris Plages' mist, cut through the Louvre.
Remembered beef tartare and Belgian ale,
the blue-gray gargoyle shade at Notre Dame,
Shakespeare and Company (I bought two books
by Arab poets). Street stalls crammed with bagged
and yellowed posters, postcards, magazines,
and photographs (Deneuve, Bardot, The Stones,
Jim Morrison, The Clash). The grip of fin
de siècle strong on streetlamps, bridges, signs,
and garrets, but the Eiffel Tower lit
at night with us inside was like a space-
ship set for lift-off. Met a coed fresh
from Indiana, traded tales until
we got her to her store-front hostel. Then
I started wanting you so badly, sweet
familiar ache that's old as pyramids
of Giza, new as pyramids designed
by Pei. Our swank hotel was steps away.

From a Garret in Paris

Hotel du Louvre

The rooftops out the bedroom window, gray
but gilded purple-gold with dawn: I need
to take a photo, but the battery
is charging. CNN's just done a piece
about a movie star who vainly peed
midflight into a bottle, missed his mark,
but made the news. These messages are to
myself; the metaphors, faint ghosts that lurk
so cheaply sheeted or ethereal
that I need say no more about them. *Stay*
in town is what I tell my wife. *Get on*
the ground and live our lives, our life. Don't try
Versailles. There's gold enough within the murk
of city shadows, shadows in ourselves.

Americans in Paris

Monet, Renoir, Cezanne, Gauguin, Van Gogh:
Impressionists and Post-Impressionists
whose works we know and love to hate—Well, no,
familiarity's contempt consists
of snobbery, in part, and "love to hate"
is a cliché, so let's just take it back
and say the paintings' colors scintillate,
their amplitude's almost sublime; our lack
of knowledge of the lesser greats—Courbet,
Signac, Corot, let's say—is humbling and
enlightening. . . . We leave Musée d'Orsay
to other tourists; take the bridge to stand
above the Seine, so old and dense, and sense
our culture's youth and brash self-confidence.

Pont du Gard

The bridge so high above the River Gard,
and we are in its plumbing: limestone eight,
eleven inches thick inside the scarred
stone throat that brought the water south, its fate
to flow—where else?—away from what resists.
Our crawling through this Roman aqueduct
is like a birth, but also death: both trysts
involve a crossing over, psyches plucked
from mist, then bathed in light, then darkness, light
again. . . . The sun and stone, the river-skin
all glint but sheathing swirling murk. The height
enough to wet our palms. The swimmers in
the distance, ants like us. Descent, like flight:
an inkling where we're going, where we've been.

From a Balcony in Nice

Hotel Negresco

Both sea and sky dream eye-white blue, and I
feel empty as these eggshells on my break-
fast plate. On TV news, twelve people die—
a high-def fire, a bomb-blast pixel-fleck
from dire Afghanistan. . . . I turn to see
two runners on the Promenade whose race
might be my higher self and I, set free
as dogs unleashed that dream a master's face
but never see it clearly, trusting scent
or intuition, knowing faintly, bent
on ecstasy, but fawning and afraid.
So many times I roll my pant-legs, wade
in shallows. I must find the pier and dive
in deep, be swallowed whole, then rise, alive.

Aquarium

Musée Océanographique de Monaco

The shark lagoon transfixed the kids and me:
the ghost-blue light in basement darkness; shrimp
among the glassed-in reefs; metallic crimp
and shimmer; fins and scales; the fishes sea-
kaleidoscoped in turquoise, yellow, red;
a moray eel with saw-tooth mouth ajar—
and then a shark would dart from overhead
or down below, the death-machine, the star-
crossed killer, silver-gilt. . . . And now? I feel
the poem's hot, quick-stinging prick and tomb-
cool burn. At sea myself, I'm bound to drown
in pixels, serifs, key-clacks, bursting creel
of psyche hooked and reeled, the bloody plume
attracting sharks, hard truths, to hunt me down.

The Guide

Musée National Message Biblique Marc-Chagall, Nice

"The closest that we get to God is when
we love another person,"
says our guide,
Chagall enthusiast, Parisienne,
who shuts her eyes to explicate
the wide
array of angels, flowers, women, goats,
and men, most bent and smiling, upside-down
or floating, flying, paired—
"And this connotes
the child-like ecstasy that even grown-
up people feel when they're in love,"
I hear
her say, her eyes still shut, so diva/muse
intense and beautiful to me
I fear
my mind's and heart's responses, think I'll lose
my bearings,
drift with figs and donkeys, steer
myself to earthy-reds, not heaven-blues.

III.

Greece

Alive and Breathing in Thessaloniki

Electra Palace Hotel

Unseen dogs barking, faint smell of diesel,
bus keen and whoosh, but lovely
white haze over the gulf, the Aegean
frosty blue despite the morning warmth.

Pigeons in Aristotle Square, unintelligible
letter combos everywhere.

White-and-black gulls swooping,
a white-and-black dog walking down below.
Raven squawks, perched on the eave above me.

Marble pillars and ledge on my balcony,
marble tile floor, wrought-iron chairs.

Motor scooter like a buzz saw.
Four barges sit in the gulf.
Blue-and-white-striped flag flutters
atop the White Tower.

Me? I'm rested and hungry,
tuning my eyes and ears for receptivity.
What does this mean? What
do I mean by "this"?

I'm alive.
I write because I want to feel alive,

want future readers (maybe only me)
to know that I have lived.

Postcards from Athens

King George Hotel

1
We shopped the Plaka after lunch, bought cheese
and apples, watched the other tourists: Turks,
Italians, Germans, and Australians.
I bought a Greek-made T-shirt saying "All
I know is that I don't know anything."
Pop Socrates, but lovely still. Tonight,
a friend recited verse from memory:
a rhyming piece he said he'd written in
his youth. Yes, this was after jugs of wine,
before the farewell hugs. All poetry.

2
It's 85 degrees at 10 a.m.,
and breakfast on the roof: white omelets, juice,
and Nescafé. Below, Syntagma Square's
ablaze. There's haze on distant mountains, haze
beyond the baked Acropolis, and haze
between my ears. Champagne and wine last night.
Hotel-room stemware roseate with dregs.
I think of Delphi, and my spirit starts
to rise. I think of all the ruins that
we've seen, and dream that I can age with grace.

Socrates Sandals

for Pantelis Melissinos

I bought a pair of sandals yesterday.
The maker was a poet, too. We swapped
each other's books; I told him where I'd stopped
along my mainland tour. I'd come to say
that poetry unites the world, but said
instead, "I've brought a gift." I realize now
the two are much the same, remember how
the sandalmaker's eyes lit up, the red
that warmed his tongue. I chose a simple pair
called "Socrates" and got the custom fit:
my naked foot was trapped, an arctic hare,
in leather strong enough to mangle it.
The maker laughed, then shaped his art: to wear
these is to walk the path of truth and wit.

Dionysus and Apollo

King George Hotel, Athens

Apollo on the Delphi mountainside,
inhaling prayers,
                    and Dionysus drunk
at Epidaurus,
                where the smallest chunk
of tragedy's so pure that kings have cried
at excess.
          I'm hung over, writing verse,
a hymn to clouds and sun that paint the sea.

(In truth, it's just my journal: poetry
might thunder from it or, like smoke, disperse.)

It's breakfast on the roof; the city roasts
like Nescafé; the Parthenon's afloat
in haze.
         Last night we drank those ouzo toasts
and then made love.
                      Today, in hills remote,
we'll visit Agamemnon's tomb,
                               the ghosts
of orgy and restraint, the throat-slashed goat.

After Visiting Mycenae

King George Hotel, Athens

King Agamemnon's tomb was cool as thought,
a shaded haven gouged in mountain, bored
within Mycenae's pocked and sun-scorched skull.
That brilliant dreamer Schliemann got it wrong,
however: neither palace, tomb, nor mask
belonged to Clytemnestra's husband, so
our local guide explained. She then curtailed
the tour because of triple-digit heat.

Now, drinking Mythos lager in an air-
conditioned room, I'm excavating words
and actions: much of life's misread. But fact
is just a tool that etches, sculpts, or dulls
realities that we ourselves create.
That tourist ouzo that I bought today:
the bottle has Apollo's Attic shape.

Note from Arachova

Santa Marina Arachova Resort and Spa

The green and black Parnassus Mountains rise
in hazy morning light above the roofs
of orange tile. A dog barks twice. My head
is clear. This is the farthest east I've been
in forty years. Wood table-top is grained
and stained as my own body is, but not
as cursed and weathered as these mountains are.
A church bell rings. A distant dog begins
to bark. The mountains bloom to pink and beige
in rising light. Dog barks again. Like me,
he's waiting for an oracle to speak.

A Note on Craft

Arachova

The sound of water trickling onto tin.
The snick of shears. A gardener. I'm at
it too: The sunrise alchemizes flat
brown-gray Parnassus rocks to coins that spin
on hems of Athens bellydancers' veils;
and bird-chirps echo off the orange tiles
of neighbors' roofs below and travel miles
beyond to snake their way through ruined trails
to kiss the ears of sibyls' ghosts that perch
on cypress-shaded stones at Delphi. Well,
that's too much noise. Be quiet. . . . Now, a bell.
A dog-bark. Clank of tools. Somewhere a church,
and workmen mending it? A hammer-blow. . . .
Which parts ring true? I'm working hard to know.

Note from the Peloponnese

Olympia Oasis Hotel

Sea pictures in my mind this morning make
me want and need to know: the boom of surf,
the breeze in leaves of trees so tropical
they'd never grow back home the birds unseen
and seen that chirp and flutter all across
the rose and green and gold foreground, the sea
Ionian, two shades of silver-blue,
the mountains hazed in pink and cream and gray. . . .

The ancient Greeks, we're told, found areté,
a kind of wisdom, courage, balance, grace,
along these shores. Olympia not far
away, its limestone dust, its shrine to Zeus
a shell, its ghosts of athletes rubbed in oil
and dirt: all found, then hidden, found again.

Mind in Flight

Lufthansa Airlines, Athens to Frankfurt to Detroit

The altitude is 40,000 feet,
we're west of Ireland, south of Iceland. Wine,
liqueur, and German beer have mixed to heat
my mind to phoenix-flight—No, not that fine:
more like a priest-drugged sibyl's, slavish-free.
A Donald Duck cartoon is playing on
the monitor: a sylvan scene, at dawn;
it could be Delphi, Epidaurus; see
the trees and stream and rocks, the absent gods.
"Shoot nature with a camera, and not
a gun," the cartoon caption reads. At odds,
the two eternals: art and death. I've got
my third merlot—but when I'm sober, home,
I'll find the grounds to fix, or burn, this poem.

The Glory That Was

Greece: morning light bled rose, then bronze, then gold
on Mount Parnassus. I was thinking of
the grassy knolls an ocean west that hold
my parents' graves, of all the dead I love.
Tragedian and archaeologist:
my Attic mode. I plumbed the dank and dark,
recorded music antic in the mist
of dream. I burned strange herbs at Delphi, spark
of perfumed prophecy. Olympia
reigned plain and fallen. Epidaurus, scoured
Mycenae powdered my ephemera
with dust of kings. Thoughts drifted, lotus-flowered,
from Alfa beer to Agamemnon's mask,
from ghosts to questions they and I would ask.

Ottoman Dreams

Bright hordes of Ottomans in northern Greece
are tramping through my frontal lobe:
The talk
in English with that Turkish student—
niece
of Istanbul, Ann Arbor merchant, smock
embroidered with barbed filigrees of East-
meets-West—
has brought them forth,
their scimitars
like rising, falling sickle moons;
the stars
of David, Bethlehem, and Yeats's beast
kaleidoscoping with them
in my mind.

In Ankara, my sister Christine born;
at Meteora, rows of skulls on shelves. . . .

A universe of birth and death:
Designed
by Allah, God, or gods?
Or picked ripe, torn
from dreams that make all people,
worlds
ourselves?

IV.

Italy

Notes from Rome

1
At the Coliseum: "They loved the blood.
Lots of it," said our Tuscan guide,
proud of his own.

Drank lots of water—
safe, we're told— from city fountains. Saw
the house where Keats died.

Had a beer,
called a grown man *signora*
at the Villa Borghese.

Everywhere, myriad depictions
of the Son of God.
I came, I saw, I didn't go bonkers.

—*Colonna Palace Hotel*

2
Horn-honks, a siren, a *beep-*
beep repeating itself. All underneath
the cicada scream.

Still on the balcony.
Haven't talked to my wife. Let her sleep.
I want to write.

A little tired, but having a good time.
The tourist's bought-and-later-paid-for
leisure life.

— *Albani Hotel*

Cypresses

Aboard a bus between the hills of Rome
and Florence, I was dozing with my wife
but heard that *cypress* means *eternal life.*
Our guide talked on; at least *one* fact hit home.
I saw the cypresses upon the hills,
like spearheads pointing heavenward, leaf-green
up close and smoke-wreathed flames of life when seen
through Tuscan haze. This dreaming vision fills
the wine-cup of the poet's mind, I think;
the lamp that hangs by golden chains above
the sculptor's stone. So Dante's verses sink
so deeply in the soul, and rays of love
revealed to toiling Michelangelo
a *David* in the marble's ageless glow.

Pisan Protest

Misión Joven Madrid, Pisa

Let the Spanish youths sing and dance
The Duomo's white as baptized souls
And so's the Tower
Leaning left if you look at it right

They sing and dance a circle dance
Wave a flag of gold and white
Two wear Spanish flags on their ass
Let them play and sing and dance

Tambourines   guitars   and congas
Pass the mic   let the younger women sing
Polizia   stay away awhile
Their Jesus placards bear no guile

The dancers circle   circle   circle
Music of the spheres circles   circles   circles
Molta bella!   My wife and I watch and smile
Oh let the *jóvenes* sing and dance awhile

Venice

Hotel Carlton

Venezia, the road signs read along
the way from fair Verona. Then, I tramped
from green canals to tourist traps: a wrong
turn here, a merchant there, the jewelry cramped
with T-shirts, shellfish, stacks of lace. I bought
three neckties: naked *David*, phallic spires,
the Lion of Saint Mark. I found a spot
beside the Grand Canal to nurse the fires
of sunburned nose and neck, to drink a cold
Peroni. On Burano Island, I
was nearly drawn into a fight: the white
wine running out, the harried waiters bold
enough to curse. I heard Pound's grave's nearby.
My own mind's drowning in its sea of night.

In the Shadow of Vesuvius

Lacryma Christi is the wine we drink:
the tears of Christ we taste before we know
the vines are grown in ash Vesuvius
has sown. Those Pompeii Romans couldn't think
dull ash, thick smoke would kill them quicker than
the ruby lava or the golden fire.
Oh, let this poem radiate beyond
this page, beyond the purring tourist bus
that took us to these ruins of the dead,
beyond our surly guide's Italian-
inflected facts; oh, let this poem, read
aloud or silently, induce, inspire
this vision of the dying and what dawned
on them: the first word after death, *Hello*.

Italian Sonnet: I Think of Us

I think of us when I remember Rome:
the Vatican, the Spanish Steps, cheap wine,
gelato at the Pantheon, the pine-
cool nights we called Colonna Palace home.

I think of us beside that Pisa dome:
the Tower leaned in sizzling light divine
as bible punishment. The anodyne?
The street musicians' riffs, Peroni foam.

I think of us in Florence: supper in
the Tuscan hills, the gruff ceramicist
who showed us his great kiln, the *David*'s poise.

I think of us adrift with mandolin
and song upon the Grand Canal: we kissed,
ignored the gondolier, the whistling boys.

Rubble-Song

The sonnet's proposition: rubble-song.
Remember the Acropolis? Our boots
that scuffed the dusty-dreaming stones? The roots
of green-speared cypress prodding Delphi's throng
of buried seers to rise from ash? A Coke
in crowded gargoyle shade at Notre Dame?
Gelato at the Pantheon? We came,
we ate, we photographed: worm-eaten joke,
guffaw among sarcophagi. "Go see
the world before your hips or knees give out,"
a graybeard told me once. A poem's no place
to die: I've heard that too. The aging face:
smile-lines run deep, the brow's well plowed by doubt.
Let's hope we're living fast but dying slowly.

V.

Great Britain

Highland Fling

Just south of Inverness, the highland hills,
like silent Easter Island monoliths,
hide buried dead that won't lie still, house ghosts
that open wounds to show us memory's bones.

And we are much like this: an iPod full
of séance voices vibrates warm as scotch
within the hidden zipper pocket of
the vest that shrouds my heart; it forks its root

to spook the sleepers in the porches of
my ears. Your jacket's blue, untimely ripped
from God's blank mind, is creasing, flapping in
this wind, a pennant on the battlements

of treason-bloodied Dunsinane. The Thane
of Cawdor must have trod these slopes before
his wild surmise began to hang its dead
weight like an albatross to drown his rest.

And so we tread them slow, but hunker now
to watch a stream as silver as a sword,
yet twisted and umbilical; it trills
and burbles down to bid us drink, forgive.

Glasgow Necropolis

Above the highway, high beyond the stained
cathedral, sits the city
we interrogate
with camera and memories
both manufactured and exotic.
Here,
we see a *THOMAS* etched into a stone,
the *T* eroding
like a soldier's face,
like neon-hued desires
the decades fade.
In grassy shade,
three gray slabs lean and show
their cracks;
they're less obscene than drunken, maid
and butlers cleaning up:
the fete
has lasted past a century.
Alive,
we're free to think such things.
And here's
another:
monuments extending skyward are
eternal lovers' fingers groping for
the hair
of God, whom all the bitter living know
is bald.
Yes, we imagine it, and it's
made real, as real as these, the dead
who now

are dancing with us,
hands so cool yet kind,
their ragged swinging hips enticing us
to lie with them,
temptation sweet as sex-
then-sleep.
We each take partners to the bus;
the tour guide needn't find them seats.

Americans in Oxford

The Old Parsonage

Our accents surely give away our roots.
In pub or hotel restaurant, our speech,
our clothes, our shoes, our skin, our builds must reach
the eyes of natives here, like hobnailed boots
identify a country rube in books
by Dickens, Hardy, Eliot. We love
the local ales, the cozy tavern nooks,
the parks, the cobblestones, the clouds above
that break to free the "English sun," a sun
our concierge suggested might not warm
our foreign bones. But these are cousins here:
we share a language and a culture dear
to us. Despite the world's sore ills that storm
and howl like Lear divided, we are one.

VI.

Conjugal Journeys

Conjugal Journeys

1. Amygdalae and Synapses

Amygdalae and synapses: you break
the music of the spheres with rack and thumb-

screw idiolect. Sounds fresh, better than tennis
without a net. Your wife reminds you, though:

the sun, the nothing new that's ever under
it. She's right: the Eiffel Tower, Bay

of Fundy, Scottish Highlands, Parthenon,
the Western world you've seen in bits and bobs.

You try to haul it in, to shore these fragments
up against your ruins. It's heroic.

And absurd. Some music makes you want
to cry: you won't. But that's another poem.

Right now, it's Brian Eno on the playlist,
reshaping ambiences you should share.

2. Badlands

These days, you feel the need to stare an animal
in the eyes. Be eaten, even. Wear

its pelt or fill its belly. No, it's not
the whiskey talking. Cabin fever, maybe.

"That buffalo was bigger than our Subaru,"
you say, your wife and you remembering

your North Dakota days. "They're bison, honey.
Look it up." You do. She's right. But so is

your urge for juices—something—flowing. Doing
evil is banal, and virtue is

a luxury. But binaries are not
enough. The landscape, mindscape, scapegoat, great

escape . . . all stark but fossil-rich, big-skyed.
You wondered how you'd finish life? Not *wise. Amazed.*

3. Camouflage

a memory   it's running with you down
the street   could be Hanoi   could be Des Moines

you're naked in the rain   or is this napalm
falling   Dad in Vietnam   mid-'60s

you're in Iowa with Mom   two younger
sisters   man of the house   with grade school eight

to three   film noir (you didn't know to name it
then) at night   a softball bat rests in

the bedroom corner   for protection   safer
than a gun   Dad brings you back a black

silk jacket   map of Thailand   Laos   Cambodia
embroidered on it   garish red and green

and yellow   stop   no   go   proceed with caution
blood   grass   sun   or   fire   envy   son

4. Green Man in the Apennines

The Apennines just north of Florence hug
their pines, he thinks, like sons about to go

to senseless war. Packed tourist buses chug
from peak of green to peak of green, and though

his thoughts are low, his rising lust peaks green,
a pagan god's. He eyes the women on

his bus: they're not the best he's ever seen,
but with one mirrored glance, his heart is gone.

Near-fifty fool! This way lies madness, sure!
Remember works of art you've seen: they scream

"Alive! Yes, I'm alive!" but murmur pure
devotion, too: to duty, not just dream.

Besides, right here's your wife. And what's ahead?
Good wine, a clean Venetian hotel bed.

5. Hauntings

That Escondido open mic: your nephew
killed it on guitar. You kept your folded

poems, pale vagina, in your pocket.
Sunburned forehead flaking snow, you're drinking

local beers you brought back warm, packed
like ingots in your dirty clothes. When flying

in and out, you saw the ocean, never
touched it. Socks got wet while walking shoeless,

drunk, in midnight rain around that gated
subdivision. Cell-phone photos just

a husk. The wispy kernel's lodged between
the ears: the hauntings of all travelers

so lightly *here*. Last morning hike, your brother's
wife said, "God, your legs are so damned white."

6. It Isn't Far

It isn't far from ear to ear, yet everything
that you can see—Loch Ness, Grand Tetons, or

Manhattan skyline—fits inside your head.
Orion strides above the arborvitae:

saw it with the dog out back. And now,
you're sitting on the couch, a second beer

half gone, your wife intently doing something
on her phone. The space between you, feet

or universes, likely worlds curved weirdly
and overlapping, ghosts commingling in

the drift. As Hamlet says, "Let be." The secret
to a happy marriage: "Keep your mouth shut":

wisdom of the elders, ancient eyes
your stars. Or did you see this on TV?

7. Meteora

The god in red, the girl in blue, and you:
the symbolism Byzantine as if

you're painted icons dancing on a cliff
that lifts these ancient monasteries to

a clearer view of heaven. Life is bright
in high Thessalian light: the mangy cur

that chases tourist buses smells of myrrh
and licks his fur to purer gold; the fright-

ful shelves of skulls throw glow like gaslit glass;
and you, in contemplation fierce enough

to wake the god and girl like April grass—
a trinity, a mystery, such stuff

that creeds are made of. Let our deaths amass:
they can't withstand true art's, pure faith's rebuff.

8. Nature Preserve

Black river cuts like glass through deep-woods pine.
You see this even from the Ford's back seat.

And later, sun-stunned aspens gird the interpretive
center. Inside, photos, maps, and taxidermy:

heron, river otter, black-bear cub.
The pelts of foxes, elk. A video

your friend has made plays on a loop: it's Bach
as background, shots of meadows, reedy ponds,

a sketch by Audubon, and interviews
with scientists now dead. Back home, your injured

dog, Elizabethan-collared, snoozes
in his crate. Your knee's still killing you,

your shoulder crackling. Hell it is, getting
old. Remember you're no better than grass.

9. Offerings

This gauze of breath, this tonic ink, this sham
career that's panacea, salve for pain;

some posturing; Neruda, Paz, Verlaine;
Pessoa, Akhmatova, Mandelstam.

Rotini pasta, Reggiano, cracked
black pepper, Kalamata olives, oil,

fresh-tossed in stoneware bowls; a beer, Crown Royal,
or last night's cabernet; clean dishes stacked.

The satin jazz of Ella, Ellington;
or Getz's bossa nova; *Kind of Blue*;

(you'll play mid-sixties Coltrane after you
have tucked her in, then join her there by one).

Manhattan, London, Athens, Rome: where you've
been lovers rediscovering your groove.

10. Second Honeymoon

The ceiling's studded like a biker's belt.
Wife's wearing white, her fetish, and she takes

a belt of what you're sipping. Now she's dancing
with a guy who has a dart stuck in

his belly. Just imagine Pap's syringe
in one of Momma's lemon-carrot Jello

molds. Today you saw two bear cubs in
a tree. Wife slipped on rocks across a stream:

you caught her, smelled her cigarette, and kissed
her quickly. Now you sing alone to "Good

ol' Rocky Top." Twelve country 8-tracks stacked
behind the bar, like tablets of the prophets.

Mountains smoked inscrutably when you
arrived. How much loss they must abide.

11. Sonnet from the Continent

Descartes is sitting in an oven big
enough to sit in, cooking up "I think;

therefore, I am"; and Plato plays his gig
inside the cave, where shadows rise and sink.

Your pages do the same. Your senses, thoughts
are drifting, kissing lips of storied shores:

Aegean, Adriatic; ouzo shots
and dry red wine, your tide. The mind adores

reminders it's alive: to feel what's felt,
to think what's thought, to write; to let the muse

assume her shapes: the succubus who's knelt
between a zealot's knees, the vestal's ruse

of gods in lieu of sex. The New World's gone,
for now. A sunset's just as bright as dawn.

12. Squeaks and Hums

A John Cage composition squeaks and hums,
a random headiness you've come to like.

The speakers, even though they're inexpensive,
aren't liars. Nor are you. It's just

that truth keeps changing. All this need, the way
that speaking clouds it. Seeing clears: a bluejay

hogs the backyard feeder, spruces suck
the filtered sun. Your slight hangover now

receding, like your hairline, like your gums.
And like the tide on Marco Island ten,

eleven New Year's Eves ago. Remember
scotch, the ocean's moan, the married sex,

collecting shells. At least you kept them zipped
in plastic. Lasted till spring cleaning came.

13. The Story of the World, Part 2

Your temples and your spirit gray with age:
the story of the world. But in the car with her,

you're bigger than a country. Road tunes from
the stereo: it's Leonard Cohen she

likes best, ambivalent, shorn, sexy, warm—
or silence's familiar rhapsody.

Slow curves, then flat-out speed through many states:
afraid, content, exhilarated, bored;

that's Texas, North Dakota, Illinois,
and Iowa. Don't try to match them up.

Keep moving. Don't discuss your future in
a parking lot. Let light and shadow blur

and flicker. Through the windows, road and sky,
field, river, fire: your will engulfs your world.

14. A Visit Home

The bare trees: needles pricking sky. The sun:
a silent uncle drunk as usual.

Let gossip spread its heady pollen, one
of many crosses people bear in full-

blown sight of others in a Catholic town
in spring. Like some, the wife has got a mum

alive and dying: ninety-one, and down
to hell she fears she'll go, chained tight and dumb.

Her son-in-law's a weirdo who descends
to nether circles, searching for a piece

of mind, of ass, of anything that bends
to fill the gap, gum up the works, release

his puzzled demons. There he sits. Observe
his grimace. Poets get what they deserve.

15. Well Enough

Your dog's got wounds he can't stop licking: much
like you. A hotel room in northern Michigan,

but could be anywhere. Your wife is in
the shower: humming, whooshing vent fan, plumbing.

You imagine other guests in flipflops, milling,
swilling lobby coffee, all self-medicating.

From his bed, the dog looks up at you,
like Adam up at God: absurd. The phone's

half-charged: you check the scores, your team blown out
again. Your life, you like it well enough.

You like it . . . Well. . . . The moon invisible
in daylight: reason blinds you sometimes. Up

to you to see tonight's sky full of scattered
stars, like salt that burns. Or that you savor.

16. Whale Watching

Bay of Fundy

The lobster-boat-turned-tourist-tub rode out
the rocking waves. Sun turned the water gray,

and shade drew out the blue some people tout
as heavenly, but you sensed danger, day

of judgment. "Don't be Jonah. Please stay in
the boat": she thinks you are the kind to dive

or fall, be swallowed whole, your qualms a skin
so easily peeled raw, to be alive

a gift you might exchange or seldom use.
"Leviathan" is what you thought, box lunch

between your feet, your camera a ruse
of rough-and-readiness. The captain's hunch

was right: you found some whales, three humpbacks and
their calves. You prayed until your feet touched sand.

17. Fellow Travelers

These sonnets, footnotes to the memoirs we
construct in dreams, sustain us on the path,

however brambled, stony, wind-lashed, bee-
loud, wild-flowered it might be. We do the math:

five beats, ten syllables, for fourteen lines.
It's walking, breathing, chanting, tapping beats

on fingers or inside the mind, cool pines
or sun-struck eagles overhead, the bleats

of sheep, the cricket-chirp for counterpoint.
The journey takes some unexpected turns.

The branches bend, reveal a roadhouse joint:
we have a beer, the shot of whiskey burns,

we have another. Stories morph and blend,
but this is just one chapter, not the end.

18. Naïve and Sentimental

This world so hard and dark but ours and shot
clean through with light—and so I write to you,

storm coming. I am drunk on life and clouds
and God—or likely, love. That's all we know

on earth. So bring the dogs, a hat, a coat,
your suffering—and come with me to . . . I

don't know, a place we make, a space, a world,
an opening in matter, stuff. I'm not

a physicist. A lover of the possible:
that's me. So loving that I break myself

for openings. Odd God, but maybe He/
She/It is in us all. Relax. Some things

stay green. And if not this, *Next world*, I say,
next world. Our changes haven't finished yet.